S
Lik
Diva

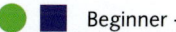

From Fear to Fun in 86 Pages

Jennifer and Jeff Bergeron

Beginner - Intermediate

Library of Congress Control Number 2007924943

ISBN: 978-0-9793223-0-3

Ski Like A Diva

Contents

about the authors/ acknowledgements

Jeff and Jennifer Bergeron

ABOUT THE AUTHORS

Jeff Bergeron, Co-author

Jeff owns Boot Fixation, a ski boot alignment business in Breckenridge, Colorado, and is widely regarded as one of the top boot technicians in the U.S. He's been working on boots since 1987 and operating his own shop since 1996.

Jeff has worked as an instructor and race coach, and is a former Regional Masters Racing Champion. When not working on boots, he can be found at his computer working on his upcoming ski books and websites. What little time is left over is reserved for fast skiing and fast cars.

Jennifer Bergeron, Co-author

Unlike the others who worked on this book, Jennifer is not addicted to skiing and has never wanted to put hours into researching her skiing issues. Her only desire was to be a confident and comfortable skier, and every book she saw seemed to be for advanced skiers who wanted a lot of technical information. She saw a need for a different kind of ski book: short, simple, and written for women who want to move past their fear to find the fun in skiing.

"My husband Jeff is not only an excellent skier but the best teacher I've ever had. However, a major difference in our ski experiences is that he doesn't understand what it's like to be afraid of anything. Whenever I happened to express a fear out loud, he would respond, 'Oh, you worry about that? Just do … ' Problem solved.

"On a hike last summer my friend Jolina Karen and I brainstormed our specific concerns about the upcoming ski season. For each one mentioned, the other one of us would say, 'Oh yeah, ask Jeff that one!' So we did. He hasn't been stumped yet."

A year later, Jolina's sketches inspired the cover illustration.

ACKNOWLEDGEMENTS

Many people volunteered their time and expertise to help us with this book, all of them acting from their shared passion for the sport. We'd like to thank the following:

Anna DeBattiste, our Ask Anna columnist, Editor and Publisher, teaches skiing at Copper Mountain Resort, and works as a freelance writer and editor during the off-season. As a Level 2 PSIA-certified instructor, she works as part of the team that runs the Women's Wednesday program at Copper, a popular weekly class for women who want to improve their skiing without being pushed beyond their comfort zone by the "testosterone crowd." She won an Instructor of the Year award in 2007 for her work with the program.

Tracy Heller, Graphic Designer, has worked in the field of publishing for 15 years. In her spare time she enjoys bookbinding and letterpress printing. She lives in Sacramento with her boyfriend, Dave, their cat, Little Man, and their whippet, Katie, the resident webmaster of www.SkinnyDogPress.com. Tracy did the cover design and layout for the book.

Peter Grannis, Photographer, has been in advertising photography in Colorado since 1987. He also ski instructs at Arapahoe Basin Ski Area. Contact him at www.asmpcolorado.org/members/grannis_peter.

Doug Lane, Photographer, has been a volunteer with the National Ski Patrol System for 27 years, and a member of the popular ski club Over the Hill Gang for three years.

Bob Barnes, Keystone Ski School's Director of Training, PSIA Examiner and Instructor Trainer, and author of The Complete Encyclopedia of Skiing. Amongst his many talents, Bob does outstanding photo work. He took the picture of Annie Black on page 77.

Annie Black, Head Coach and Trainer for Keystone's Betty Fest™ Women's Ski Program, longtime PSIA Examiner and Instructor Trainer, and Colorado Ski Country's 2006-07 Instructor Of The Year.

Sarah Chevalier, Ski Instructor, contributed content for the Ask Anna sections and modeled for some of the ski technique photos. An Australian who began her teaching career in New Zealand in the 1980's, Sarah is a passionate skier who has taught in resorts all over the world.

Katy Perrey, Ski Instructor for Copper Mountain Resort, contributed content for Ask Anna and modeled for some of the ski technique photos. Katy has been teaching for 18 years and is fully certified by PSIA (Professional Ski instructors of America) as well as having a children's accreditation. She has been named among Skiing Magazine's Top 100 Instructors.

Heather Quarantillo, Co-foreman of the Women's Wednesday Program at Copper Mountain Resort, is also fully certified and has taught for ten years. She specializes in private lessons and has a children's accreditation. In her spare time, she enjoys ski racing, competitive trail running and sailboat racing. She contributed content for the Ask Anna sections.

Ski Like A Diva

introduction

Successful women are used to being in control of their lives. There is a plan for keeping the career focused, the family organized, the bills paid, exercise done, the house neat, meals planned, friends seen and challenges met. Women set the bar high for themselves and often succeed not only at meeting their goals, but even surpassing them.

Skiing is not difficult, but living up to unrealistic expectations is. The fear and frustration you experience with a new physical endeavor, especially if you're taking it on because of encouragement (or pressure) from someone who is already an expert, is very real. We encourage you to admit that fear rather than ignore it; then learn what to do about it. Admitting it alone is a success, and a huge relief! **You're going to learn to use fear to your advantage.**

Learn how to be comfortable, how to avoid danger, and most importantly, how to have a really great time out there!

"Let's go skiing right now!"

–Roald Amundsen, Norweigan Explorer of the Antarctic

chapter 1

Take the Pressure Off – Fear is OK

"To use fear as the friend it is, we must retrain and reprogram ourselves ... We must persistently and convincingly tell ourselves that the fear is here—with its gift of energy and heightened awareness—so we can do our best and learn the most in the new situation."

**–Life 101 by Peter McWilliams,
New York Times Bestselling Author**

"Fear grows in darkness; if you think there's a bogeyman around, turn on the light."

**–Dorothy Thompson,
American Journalist**

"I discovered I scream the same way whether I'm about to be devoured by a Great White or if a piece of seaweed touches my foot."

**–Kevin James, Actor,
"The King of Queens"**

Too often, women skiers' single biggest problem **is not the mountain or terrain, but the pressure they put on themselves**.

On the surface, this pressure is not easy to see. You may say things like, "I'm just here to have fun," or "I just want to have a good time," but this is not the full story. Underneath, you have bigger expectations: "as long as I look good on the slopes, as long as I have complete control, as long as I look like I know what I'm doing, *then* I'll have fun."

Give yourself a break. You're not here to perform. Take the easy run if you feel like it. Laugh a little if you make a mistake. Soak in the fresh mountain air. Have some cocoa just because you want to.

Remember, **you are skiing—let the "superwoman" stay at home**.

FEAR IS NOT A BAD WORD

> *"Maybe women get scared more because they have better sense and are smarter than men."*
> *– A friend's 78-year-old mother*

A lot of women get mad at themselves for being frightened when they're struggling with a harder trail. They seem to think they have to defeat their fear. They're missing the point: fear protects you.

Rather than trying to defeat fear, accept it as part of skiing. Rather than working your way down a difficult mogul run, enjoy making gentle turns instead. Not forcing progress is the easiest path to success and improvement.

When you think about it, people are not really made to fly down a mountain on sliding planks. Tackling a green run is a major accomplishment. So begin each day by keeping everything easy and see the good in what you can do. By reaching a level of acceptance, you'll have more fun and find it *much easier to progress*.

Ask Anna

Q: I want us to ski as a family on our vacation but we're all at different levels. How can we bring it together to have shared time?

A: Everyone needs to be in agreement that the point of the trip is to enjoy time as a family. Each day, plan a certain time to meet on the hill. Spend an hour dedicated to each other. This means that everyone waits, and encourages and enhances each others' experience. If ski abilities are very different, it's impractical to force everyone to stick together all the time. Taking the pressure off applies to everyone in the group. There is enough stress from being in unfamiliar territory without creating more due to unreachable expectations.

Ask Anna *cont.*

Taking lessons can help. Some resorts offer family privates, and these can work well for a family that wants to ski together and is willing to be patient with everyone's different abilities. A good instructor can keep everyone challenged by moving between family members and juggling different task assignments. If the pace is still too varied, however, the best thing is to let everyone ski on their own and arrange certain times throughout the vacation to meet for lunch or for a run or two.

chapter2

Equipment Is Important

"I'm an average skier so my average equipment is fine. When I get better I'll buy better stuff."
–Jennifer Bergeron

It's easy to blame yourself for problems you're not even causing. You'll run into trouble by trying to force the wrong equipment to do something it can't do. A common problem caused by improper equipment is skiing in the "backseat," with your center of mass *behind* rather than *over* your feet. Because women have a different center of mass than men, men's skis and boots don't work the same way for them. Women generally have longer legs relative to the torso length and less mass in the torso.

In an ideal world your equipment would be set up for this difference, but it rarely is. "Women's skis and boots" may simply mean men's equipment with minor tweaks and different colors. Out of the box, most ski equipment is essentially set up for men.

Fortunately, some shops are aware of what women need and they address it. Good boot shops will perform alignment work that can offer the greatest advantage. If you're having a ski problem you cannot seem to beat, have the equipment looked at by a skilled professional.

Don't ignore the benefits of the smallest advantages. Sometimes, the little things count most. Because you must deal with so many issues in skiing—cold weather, slippery slopes, unfamiliar ski shops, etc.—**everything you can do to improve your state of mind and body is important.**

Ask Anna

Q: Will I know if it's my equipment or me?

A: If you're a new skier, probably not. The best thing to do is to start with the right equipment. If you continue to struggle with one issue as the rest of your skiing improves, try another pair of skis, have your alignment re-checked and get your skis tuned.

For more experienced skiers, there are some signs of equipment deficiency you may recognize. Your foot shouldn't move excessively in any direction and your calf shouldn't be pinched. Women's calves are typically lower than men's, and most women's boots are made with a lower cuff to accommodate this. Don't let anyone tell you that foot pain is just a part of skiing; it shouldn't be. Skis should be fairly short, and unless you are a very advanced skier or a racer, you should avoid skis that are heavy or stiff.

chapter 3

Tips Specifically for Beginners

"You can learn new things at any time in your life if you're willing to be a beginner. If you actually learn to like being a beginner, the whole world opens up to you."

—Barbara Sher,
Career Counselor and Bestselling Author

Skiing is fun, exciting, healthy and scary in a good way. If you've never skied before and want to get started, there are a few keys to make your first experience safe and enjoyable.

- **Take a lesson from a pro** – For the first-time skier, *a professional lesson is a must.* You aren't learning just one skill, but a few basic skills and how to put them together. Only a professional instructor has the training to make this process as relaxed, simple and safe as possible. You can often request a specific instructor for a lesson. See the instructor section for more on this.

- **Ski on a nice day** – Learning to ski is easier if you're not dealing with a blizzard. If the day you plan to start turns out to be minus 40 degrees and snowing, consider skipping it and going the next day. If you can't avoid the weather because of a timed vacation, be ready to take breaks often. If you're warm and happy you'll have a great time in the falling snow, sometimes even a better time than you would have had on a clear, sunny day.

- **Rent *short* skis** – Start with skis shorter than 150 centimeters (cm). Generally, lengths between 120 and 140 cm are best for your first time. It is better to wait to buy skis and boots until after your first few days. Your skis will look different than what a lot of other people are using, but you'll know that you're on the right ski for you, and that makes you smart and prepared.

- **Read the rest of this book** – The tips in this book apply to beginners and experienced skiers alike.

Ask Anna

Q: Can an adult really learn how to ski if they've never ever done it before?

A: Yes! Many people learn to ski as adults. Although you may have more fear to overcome than those who started skiing as children, you still have the same opportunities to develop your skill level. And in fact, you may develop your appreciation of the sport far more than those who have grown up with it.

The best way to have an experience you want to repeat is to take a lesson your first time. The instructor can make sure you have the right equipment, are on the appropriate terrain, and learn the skills you need to make it fun.

chapter 4

The Six Most Common Reasons People Don't Ski and What to Do About it

1 I'm freezing and I've only been here five minutes.

"Cold! If the thermometer had been an inch longer we'd have frozen to death."

–Mark Twain, Humorist, Writer and Lecturer

What good are shaped skis and high speed lifts if you're cold and miserable? No good at all, of course! Cold skiing is miserable skiing, so staying warm is job one – even more important than your technique or ski equipment. Women tend to get cold quickly, and their bodies are generally designed to keep their circulation at the core.

1. **Keep your feet warm; few things are worse than skiing in cold, wet boots.**

   - *Wear dry wool socks, not too thick* – Modern wool socks are warm, absorbent, and don't itch. Ideally they should have a high Merino wool content (over 90%). If you don't like wool, wear silk or polypropylene. Avoid socks that are too thick because they bunch up and block circulation. Thicker does not mean warmer.

Recommended brands: Smartwool, DeFeet

- *Dry and warm your boots overnight* – To avoid cold and wet boots, let them dry out after a day of skiing before you go out again. Use a heated boot dryer, which most shops sell. (Some are too hot for your custom footbeds and will melt them, so use caution.) Another option is to pull your liners out of your boots for the night. One more thing – never leave your boots in the car!

- *Get boot heaters* – If your feet are always cold, consider getting electric boot heaters installed. New heaters are well built and do a great job of taking the bite out of the cold.

  Recommended brand: Hotronic

2. **Most heat is lost through your head and hands, so keep them well protected.**

   - *Helmets and hats (and headbands)* – Helmets and hats will keep you much warmer than if you leave your head bare. A helmet is the best option, providing warmth, airflow and protection. Most shops even rent them, if you want to try before you buy. If you aren't ready for a helmet, wear a hat instead for the extra warmth. The last option is to use a headband, which can still add quite a bit of warmth. Stay warm and know you're ready for the elements.

   - *Gloves and mittens* – Gloves offer dexterity and mittens offer more warmth, so go with your preference. Glove liners and heat packs can add warmth, too. *SUPER SECRET TRICK* – If you use heat packs, shake them to get them up to temperature before going outside.

Recommended brand: Thinsulate brand insulation works well for warmth. Swany TOASTER series of gloves and mittens can be zipped open so you can add a heat pack. Some of their mittens also have an attached glove liner that can be used for handling smaller items, such as keys.

Heat pack brand: HotHands-2 work well, as do many other brands.

3. **Clothing**

Remember these words: waterproof, breathable and layers.

- *Water and wind resistance* – Jackets and pants that are treated to withstand windy, cold, damp conditions will keep you much warmer and dryer than those that aren't.

  Recommended brands: Gore-Tex and Entrant

- *Breathability* – Treated clothing will also allow good airflow. Essentially, the water outside stays out (such as snow), but the moisture from your body can still escape.

- *Layering* – What you wear underneath the jacket and pants counts too. Long underwear has improved dramatically from the old days of cotton and wool. Consider fleece types of underwear for extra warmth. Use a turtleneck or neck gator (like a scarf but with no extra length—you slip it on over your head) to keep wind from getting next to your skin and down your jacket.

- *Fit and range of motion* – Your ski clothes should be snug enough that they don't feel baggy, but roomy enough to allow you full range of motion. To test a new outfit, try wearing all of your under layers with the outer layers. You should be able to cross your arms easily, and be able to get into a full squat.

- *Bright colors* – Colors are an important part of safety. Good, visible options are oranges, reds and yellows, although any bright color works better than white or gray.

4. Go inside

Even with the best clothes and accessories, you can still get cold. Rather than ignoring your impending misery, go inside for a few minutes, warm up and re-group.

- *Drink something warm* – Tea, hot apple cider, coffee and hot cocoa are great ways to warm up from the inside out.

- *Watch what you eat* – Here's some good news: to stay warm and keep your energy up, increase your caloric intake a bit. A light salad at lunch is probably not going to be enough. But don't overdo it either; if you do have a bigger meal, give yourself a few minutes (15 to 30) to digest it before getting back on the slopes.

- *Feel justified* – Don't fight the cold when a quick break could help you warm up and will sustain a good day on the hill.

- *Dealing with altitude* – Drink a lot of water and avoid alcohol and caffeine. If you feel lightheaded, dizzy and/or nauseous, go to the nearest medical center for attention. Altitude sickness is to be taken very seriously.

Ski Like A Diva

Taking a break

2 There's so much gear and planning involved with skiing; it's difficult to stay calm and organized.

"It has long been my belief that in times of great stress, such as a four-day vacation, the thin veneer of family wears off almost at once, and we are revealed in our true personalities."
—Shirley Jackson, Author

"No one needs a vacation more than the person who just had one."
—Unknown

Taking the family skiing
can be fun!

Ski Like A Diva

> *"Well, The Dirty Dozen was like a vacation."*
> **– Clint Walker, Actor**

It used to be simple: you went to the parking lot and walked a few feet to the ski area. If you needed rental equipment, you did it at the base. They didn't have anything fancy, but it was easy.

Today, pre-skiing is different. Many ski areas have gotten HUGE! The old parking lots are gone, now covered with condos. New parking lots can literally be miles from the base area. Rather than needing just a trail map, you now need a map to get to the lifts!

Families bear the brunt of these changes; kids trudging down the icy path with oversized boots, usually crying, and Mom and Dad carrying four or five sets of equipment while trying to get their kids to lessons on time.

It's understandable that by the time you get to the ski area, you're worn out. Here are a few tips for getting to the mountain fresh and ready to ski.

- *Get a map before you go* – When you're booking a vacation, get the ski area or lodging company to send you a map of the ski area base or find it online. This map should cover where you're staying, which part of the ski area you want to go to and which buses you'll need to catch. Ideally, it will include where you'll rent skis and where you can store them.

- *Get to know the ski area before you hit the slopes* – If you arrive a day before your scheduled ski days begin, walk around the night before. If not, consider taking the first morning off and walk around the ski area's base. If possible, take the buses you will need, too.

- *Ski in, ski out* – When possible, stay as close as you can to the areas you will ski.

- *Don't walk in ski boots; use the lockers* – Walking in ski boots while carrying ski equipment is one of the biggest discomforts you can experience, and yet few skiers realize it can be avoided. Use the ski check at the base area. Use the boot check, too, if it is warm and has a boot drying feature. If necessary, store the skis and carry your boots. If you must carry all of your gear, wear shoes and carry your boots (put the straps over your ski poles).

- *Ask for help* – If you're struggling to balance your equipment and yourself *and* climb the bus steps, ask someone to give you a hand. People are happy to assist, give advice, and provide lunch tips or general information. Many ski areas now use guides who can be identified by their uniforms to give people exactly this kind of help.

- *Beat or out-wait the crowds* – Especially for busy holiday periods, try to avoid the crowds. While times can vary, the best blocks to avoid are:

     Base area between 10:00 a.m. and 11:00 a.m.

     Cafeteria and restaurants from 11:45 a.m. to 1:15 p.m.

     Rental shops from 8:30 a.m. to 10:00 a.m.

     Ski schools are often less busy for afternoon lessons.

Ski Like A Diva

Learn the easy way to carry your skis!

If you're an early riser, try to beat the rush. If you sleep a little later, or got in late the night before, try getting out after these times. The slopes are usually the least crowded between 2:00 and 4:00 p.m.

• *How to carry your gear* – Don't walk in your ski boots if you can help it. Put the boots' Velcro straps together (most boots have them; if not, use a boot handle), and slide your poles underneath the Velcro straps. Then put the poles over your shoulder, with the boots towards your back. Then put your skis over the other shoulder, *with the tips in front*. When you get to the lodge, use a locker for your shoes.

3 I'm afraid of losing control or getting hurt.

"I thought I was in control. But ...I lost it."
–Pedro Martinez, Pitcher, NY Mets

If you spend a lot of energy worrying about losing control and crashing, you're not alone. The common scenario: get scared, panic, struggle to move, get mad at yourself for being afraid, mad at struggling and mad at not being in control. Repeat. It's time to end this cycle of defeat!

An interesting contradiction in feeling unprepared is that you often have the skills to do what you want to do. But experience has taught you to be afraid. It may be that you feel you don't have the raw strength to easily regain balance once you lose it. Maybe you crashed before and it hurt. Or you got into terrain that was beyond your abilities and you had no idea what to do. These are real fears based on real situations. You're not stuck there and you can learn to handle anything once you know how to break it down.

SIX STRATEGIES FOR CONQUERING THE FEAR YOU'VE FELT BEFORE:

* *Look for small challenges* – Too often, people feel like they need to go for the big challenges and ski the steepest, iciest bump run on the mountain. Or someone told you how great the trees were and you want to keep up and experience it as well. Slow down! Instead of getting in over your head, find small challenges. Instead of taking on an entire mogul run, ski the last six moguls at the bottom of a slope. Rather than take the chair lift to the most difficult terrain, take a small step up in terrain. Overall, the best way

to build your confidence is one small step at a time. Then celebrate the success, whether it happens on the 9th or the 90th try.

- *Ski the terrain you like, not the terrain you want to like* – Sure, challenges are good for a person, but there is nothing wrong with skiing where you're comfortable. Instead of spending half your day trying to handle some bump run that's driving you crazy, why not spend most of your day on the terrain you like. A good plan is to spend 10% of your ski day on challenges, and the other 90% where you feel your best. Simply put, don't scare yourself when you could be having fun.

- *Ski for short periods of time* – Skiing for too long is fatiguing, which saps your control and greatly increases your chances of crashing. High speed lifts allow you to ski more runs now than in the old days. For the same amount of time that you may have skied in the past, you're skiing a lot more runs. If you get tired, either take a break or call it a day.

- *Use good equipment* – Don't underestimate how much control you get from good equipment. This is especially true with women's ski boots that have a basic men's design. In most cases, good alignment work can provide vastly better control and balance, such as getting you out of the "backseat."

- *Use a guide or take a lesson* – If you're new to a ski area, learning the layout of the mountain will skyrocket your comfort level. Guide services are relatively new, and often provided free of charge. You don't have to be an expert to take advantage of it. These professionals do the job they do because they like to share the mountain with newcomers and show them how to enjoy their day.

Spending a full or half day with an instructor not only increases your skill level but allows you to leave the lift line navigation, map reading and agenda to a professional. You can relax and soak in the benefits of being on the hill.

- *Work on your technique and/or take a lesson* – Even a few tips that improve your technique, therefore comfort level, go a long way toward building your confidence on the slopes.

What if you don't want to ski alone, but everyone around you is better and faster?

- *Start first* – In most groups, the fastest person starts down the hill first, and the slowest goes last. Of course the faster skiers feel like they are always waiting (and that makes them want to ski faster), and the slowest person feels like she is holding back the group and never gets a chance to rest. Instead, have the slowest skier start first with the faster skiers following. The faster skiers must give plenty of room when they pass.

- *Learn to ski faster on the flats* – Often, the biggest speed differences are on the flattest and easiest part of the hill. Assuming your ski companions are skiing at a safe speed, you should be able to increase your speed here with comfort and control. Consider taking a lesson to improve your speed on the flats. Be sure to tell the ski school what you're trying to learn before joining the lesson.

Ask Anna

Q: What can I do if I get in over my head and find myself on a slope that I simply cannot handle?

A: It's important to learn basic skills such as side slipping, downhill stepping, traversing and kick-turning to handle steep terrain. But even more importantly, try to prevent this situation from occurring in the first place. Study a trail map, and learn to follow trail signs that will get you around safely. Taking a lesson on your first day is a good way to learn where the most appropriate terrain for your ability is, and also how to read terrain so you can anticipate a steep run before you're stuck on it. Many mountains also have guides or "ambassadors" that offer mountain tours at no charge.

Most importantly, avoid following the friend who says, "Come on! I know you can handle it." Make your own decisions about terrain.

4 I don't have the right equipment.

"Proper preparation prevents poor performance."
– Charlie Batch, Quarterback, Pittsburgh Steelers

Too often, women downplay the need for good equipment. One reason that sounds valid is, "I'll get better gear when I get better." This could be the cause of most of your discomfort, both physical and mental.

Intermediate equipment is designed for intermediate skiing. It will not give you the control you need to improve. Skiing on this gear is simply the fast track to becoming a "terminal intermediate."

In order to get better, to make improvements, to have better control and to feel natural on the slopes, you need good gear.

EIGHT KEYS TO GETTING GEAR THAT WORKS FOR YOU:

- *Go short with your skis – really short.* Modern, short skis are easy to use and inspire confidence. If your skis are longer than 160 cm, try going shorter. We've seen beginner to intermediate women learn best with skis between 145 and 160 cm long.

- *Demo before you buy* – Would you buy a car without taking it for a test drive first? Of course not, so why buy a ski without trying it first? The fact is that every type of ski has its own personality, and the only way to know if it truly works for you is to try it. This "try before you buy" program is called demo-ing, and is done at most higher-end ski shops (especially those near ski areas). Typical costs for demo-ing skis are between $30 and $45 per day, and will often be applied to the purchase cost of the skis. Many shops will even let you try multiple pairs of skis after you return the first pair. Ski instructors will know good places to demo skis on each mountain.

- *Watch the weight of the skis and bindings* – Some ski/binding combinations are relatively light, while others are very heavy. By choosing a lightweight setup, you can avoid a lot of excess fatigue, ultimately resulting in better, more confident skiing. Note – use the retail models, not the demos, for weight comparisons. Most demo skis use heavier bindings that will skew the results.

- *Get the right boots – with alignment!* – So many women skiers Jeff works with are shocked to find out how bad their boots are for them, although the same boot could work for a man perfectly. Don't let the color of the boot alone convince you that a boot is shaped for what you specifically need as a woman skier. The difference between good, well-aligned boots and so-so boots is like night and day.

  Well-aligned boots will provide a strong stance, work as part of your body, and stay reasonably warm and comfortable. Ill-fitting or poorly- and non-aligned boots can ruin your skiing by limiting control, hurting or chilling your feet, and forcing an awkward stance that will throw off every aspect of balance.

  Typical boot problems for women include boots that are too loose in the heel and boots that cause fore/aft balance problems. Ski boots are complex, so choosing the right boot technician is as important as choosing the right boot. The right tech will be knowledgeable, easy to understand and committed to improving your skiing experience.

- *Get your skis tuned* – For the best ski control, use skis that are tuned and sharp. (See Getting the Right Ski Tune on page 61 for more information on ski tuning.)

- *Don't forget the ski poles* – Ski poles are essential for rhythm once your skiing advances from the beginner level. For beginners, you won't use your poles right away, but you should get accustomed to holding them while you ski; they'll also come in handy for moving you along on the flats and in lift lines. The best ski poles are light, sized properly and easy to plant. To size poles, you should hold the pole upside down and grip the shaft below the basket. If the pole is right for you, your arm will form a right angle, with your forearm parallel to the floor. The shop employee can help you make this assessment.

- *Get the right goggles (or sunglasses)* – For both sun protection and for keeping snow and debris out of your eyes, eyewear is key. For the best protection from the wind, use goggles. If you don't want to use goggles for some reason, sunglasses are better than nothing. Get lenses that have a medium tint so that you can see well on both overcast and bright days. Skiing at night will only work with clear or very lightly tinted lenses. Goggles and sunglasses come in many shapes and sizes, so try a number of them before you buy to get the right fit.

- *Wear a watch* – You will be more independent if you know how much time you have before meeting someone and you can relax without worrying about finding clocks to check.

Ask Anna

Q: I've heard something about "Q-Angle" and that it's a big deal for women. What is it, what does it do, and how does one deal with it?

A: Q-Angle is a term used to describe how the femur does not run vertically from the hip, but instead tends to run at an angle, with the knees closer together than the hips.

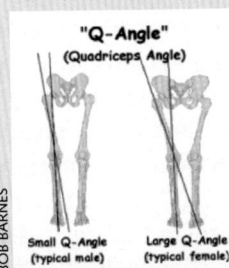

"Q-Angle"
(Quadriceps Angle)

Small Q-Angle
(typical male)

Large Q-Angle
(typical female)

BOB BARNES

Women tend to have more Q-Angle than men, which can give them a knock-kneed or A-framed stance. This can make it more difficult for a woman to put her skis on edge or to flatten them completely.

The best way to deal with a pronounced Q-Angle is to have the alignment of your ski boots checked by a high quality shop. Ski instructors and racers often know of good places to have alignment work done. A good instructor can also help with developing your technique to work with a pronounced Q-Angle.

Ask Anna

Q: I've heard people mention they brought the wrong colored goggle lenses for the day. What's the difference between the pink, yellow and clear lenses? Do I need all three?

A: Goggles are a personal choice, so it really comes down to finding out what works best for you. A woman who wants to buy just one pair of goggles should opt for a rose or amber lens. These are the most versatile, although they may not perform as well as a specific darker or lighter lens for extreme sun or flat light. A woman who struggles with vision in flat light situations should invest in a good low light lens which helps to provide maximum contrast in conditions where everything looks the same. A pair of sunglasses is a great thing to carry in an extra pocket if light conditions change drastically.

 People ski or ride too close for comfort.

"No one goes there anymore — it's too crowded."

—Yogi Berra, Former Major League Baseball Catcher and Manager

It's not your imagination; there are collisions and close calls between skiers and skiers, skiers and boarders, and boarders and boarders. High speed lifts put far more skiers on a hill, slopes get crowded, and some skiers and boarders are not as careful or as considerate as you may like.

Ski Like A Diva

TEN STRATEGIES FOR PROTECTING YOUR SAFETY ZONE

- *Use a steady rhythm* – By skiing with a smooth and steady rhythm, the skiers behind you can predict your path and avoid you. Quick, erratic moves give no warning of where you are headed. Relax into your pattern and be consistent with it.

- *Short turns* – Because you use less space on the hill and will be better able to keep your speed down, make short turns. They're especially helpful for times when the slopes are crowded.

- *Bright colors* – Skiers have to see you to avoid you. Oranges, reds and yellows are generally visible in all weather conditions.

- *Wear a helmet* – Helmets are good for both your safety and, consequently, your confidence. A helmet will also help keep you warm. If you don't own one, rent one.

- *Beat the crowds* – By skiing either early or late, you can often avoid many of the crowds. For early risers, try to be ready to ski as soon as the lifts open. Avoiding the crowds is especially important if you ski at peak times such as holidays and weekends.

- *Ski in the gaps* – Like car traffic moving along a highway, skier traffic often moves down a hill in clusters. Ski in-between these clusters and you will have more of the slope to yourself.

- *Stay towards the side (but leave a little room)* – Most skiers ski down the middle of the slope, so avoid it by skiing closer to the sides. Often, the snow will be better too. Always leave a bit of room between yourself and the trees, however, so that faster skiers can get by you, and you can avoid the trees.

- *Use Slow Zone/controlled speed areas* – Many ski areas now have what they call "Slow Zones," which are trails where only slow skiing is allowed. In theory, you should not get "buzzed" by faster skiers. Some slow zones are misnamed or over-used, so use your judgment when relaxing your guard.

- *Stay away from the "funnels"* – "Funnels" are where many ski trails merge into one trail, so they tend to get crowded and are therefore potentially dangerous. The worst kind of funnels are where novice and expert trails merge, because you get a mix of fast and slow skiers. Avoid these "funnels" if at all possible.

- *If you do get buzzed* – If you get the nerve knocked out of you because of someone getting too close, or you accidentally get too close to someone else, take a breather. Ski to the side of the run, where you are visible but out of the way of traffic, and get your breath back. Focus again on the intention of your day and get back into the fun of things.

Ask Anna

Q: What should I do if I *am* involved in a crash?

A: Your first priority is to assess whether you should move. If you feel any numbness or strange sensations in your extremities, or especially in your back or neck, stay still. Take things slowly, and don't force yourself to get up right away. Next, if you determine that you or another party is injured, place your skis uphill from the injured party and cross them. This is a universal signal for an injured skier. If you are the one who is injured, call to a passing skier or someone else in your party to do this. Then find a way to call the ski patrol.

Carry a cell phone and program the mountain's ski patrol number into it. If a cell phone is not an option, most mountains have ski patrol phones located in various places throughout the resort, or you can call to a passing skier to notify ski patrol once they reach the bottom of the mountain.

Try to remember everything that happened leading up to the accident, as the ski patroller who responds to your call will need to make a detailed report. He or she will also take care of administering first aid, and transporting you or any other injured skier to the bottom of the mountain to get appropriate medical attention.

6 I want to look like I know what I'm doing.

"If you have no confidence in self, you are twice defeated.... With confidence, you have won even before you have started."

–Marcus Tullius Cicero, Lawyer and Philosopher of Ancient Rome

While few people ski just to buy the latest fashions, skiing has always had a certain mystique and appeal to it. In the old days, there were photos of movie stars skiing and getting tanned. Then there were stretch pants, and scenes in James Bond movies. It seemed that skiing could make nearly anyone glamorous.

The biggest fear out there is the fear of looking stupid. With enough falls resulting in skewed goggles, tired technique and discouraged attitudes, even the best-looking skier can look like a tornado just hit.

FIVE TIPS TO KEEP THE CHIC

- *Have nice, not necessarily expensive, clothing* – Neatly styled, well-fitting ski clothing will make any skier look better and feel comfortable. Buy according to fit and what you like.

- *Carry your skis correctly* – Skis should be carried over your shoulder, with the *tips in front*. This isn't just a rule of fashion. It takes less effort than carrying skis upside down.

- *Relax with proper breathing* – In order to look comfortable, you must be comfortable. By using simple breathing techniques (see page 72), you can feel your best before, during and after skiing.

- *Prepare for being outside all day, and looking like it* – Hair will get flattened under a helmet or hat and snow goes everywhere, including inside your goggles. You're going to look different than when you head to the office and that's part of the fun of being out there.

- *Most people are thinking about themselves* – Remember that people pay far more attention to themselves than to anyone else. You wouldn't care so much about what other people were thinking about you if you realized how much they weren't.

chapter**5**

How to Train Your Ski Partner

(or Husband/Boyfriend Turned Ski Coach)

"My boyfriend's idea of a lesson was to take me on a black diamond run in the middle of a hail storm and say, 'Go!' Ski patrol had to escort me to another lift to get me down the mountain. No, that wasn't humiliating, not at all."

— Claudia Black, Australian Actress

"My wife did such a great job training me that I hardly remember how she did it. She even led me to believe that I came up with all these ideas on my own."

—Jeff Bergeron

TIPS FOR SUCCESSFULLY SKIING WITH YOUR PARTNER

- **Don't fight fire with fire** – Instead of throwing insults due to frustration, state what you need. If you're struggling, need alone time, or need some simple support, say it. That may mean that you want him to stop "helping" and meet you at the bottom of the hill. Even expressing, "I'm finding this really hard right now and I need your support" can change the mood of the entire run. Or start the conversation with, "I really want to enjoy skiing, but I need your help getting there."

- **When in doubt, don't do it** – Be wary if you hear a phrase like, "I think you can handle this hill." Do *not* get talked into skiing anything you don't feel safe doing, even if it means you have to take a different route down. If your partner has to do it, offer to meet him at the bottom. You can still encourage him, and you can pump yourself up for your run and look forward to sharing stories when you reunite.

- **Give each other alone time** – If you and your partner ski at different levels, take time to ski without each other. Set a time and place to meet, and ski for an hour at your individual paces. You will both have renewed patience when you meet again. If you don't like to ski alone, take a break or join a lesson. Women's ski seminars are ideal for finding people who have similar goals.

Ski Like A Diva

- **Don't learn to ski from your husband/boyfriend** – Lessons are a lot more pleasant than on-hill arguments, so unless your partner is a professional instructor, avoid it.

- **Compromise** – If a partner is insistent that you try a tougher hill (and you *are* interested in the challenge), look for a compromise. Instead of doing a whole mogul slope, find a slope where you can cut in near the bottom and ski the last seven or eight moguls. Short but steep sections can also be a great challenge.

chapter **6**

Finding the Right Instructor

"The mediocre teacher tells. The good teacher explains. The superior teacher demonstrates. The great teacher inspires."
— **William Arthur Ward, U.S. College Administrator**

KNOW THE ANSWERS TO WHAT SKI SCHOOL WILL ASK

Whether you are with the ski school front desk or looking for a referral from someone on the chairlift, you'll need to have a sense of how you currently ski and what you want to learn.

- **What terrain do you ski?**
  Never skied before (beginner)
  Green slopes (novice)
  Blue slopes (intermediate)
  Black slopes (expert)

- **Do you feel in control there?** Usually, sometimes, or "I'm scared and feel out of control!"

- **Is your main focus getting over fear or developing better skills?** It's all related, but each goal has a difference in focus. Your instructor will know whether to focus more on pace and confidence or on technical issues.

- **What do you want to gain from this lesson?** If you want to ski green runs and relax, tell them. There's nothing wrong with that as a goal. If you want to master double black diamond bump runs, say so. All the information you can provide describing what you want, helps the instructor focus on your goals.

- **Learning style** – Let the ski school or instructor know if you like to work at a hard or easy pace, if you want to repeat a drill again and if you need encouragement rather than instruction.

PRIVATE OR GROUP LESSONS?

Know how to make the right choice based on what you want to learn.

- **Private lessons** – You have the instructor to yourself for a set time (usually from an hour to all day). You will receive undivided attention and you can work at whatever pace suits you best. The cost is more than for a group lesson (often around $500 for a full day), and it isn't as social as a group lesson. Also, you can usually request a particular instructor for a private lesson, as long as that instructor is not already booked.

- **Group lessons** – Groups are usually eight people or fewer, and generally cost under $100 for a full day. If you thrive on group camaraderie and support, this may be your best option for learning. As in any classroom situation, everyone adjusts to the group's pace. You also don't get the individual attention you would from a private. Class size can vary greatly. Often, the more advanced groups have significantly fewer people, while the beginner classes —especially during the holidays—can have 15 or more students. Note that due to scheduling issues, it is often not possible to request a certain instructor for a group lesson. (Still, there is no harm in trying.)

- **Women's seminars** – Seminars are great. They typically last two or more days and have a relaxed, friendly atmosphere. You're with the same people for consecutive days so the friendships and encouragement you experience are refreshing. Groups are formed by matching everyone's goals and moving at an even pace. Finding the right seminar takes planning. They aren't generally held every day or week.

- **Women's Wednesdays and other weekly programs** – These are weekly group lessons for women that are now featured at many ski areas. Like the women's seminars, they provide a great opportunity to ski with like-minded peers. They also tend to be quite economical, and can usually be purchased either by the day or by the season.

How to evaluate your instructor: It's important to make sure you're getting what you're looking for.

- **Patience and encouragement** – The only way you can learn properly is if you feel safe, comfortable and supported. If you leave the class feeling tense and rushed, the lesson is not likely to sink in.

- **Keeping it simple** – While technique can get complicated, a good instructor can make learning simpler and easier with his/her tips. If you leave the lesson confused, it was not simple enough.

- **Limited information** – Good instructors know that too much information can be worse than too little information. An instructor should not teach more

Women's seminars and weekly group lessons are becoming very common than two unrelated skills in a lesson. This would be a "shotgun approach," in which something might hit the target but nothing is focused.

- **Retention** – When the class is finished, you should be able to use your new skills fairly well. If you cannot remember the lesson, or cannot do the new skill without the instructor, the lesson did not stick as well as it should.

- **Was it fun?** – A good instructor will show you how to have fun learning how to become a better skier.

Occasionally change instructors. Even when you have an exceptional instructor, it is sometimes good to shake things up a bit and take a lesson from someone else. Even if each one covers the same subject, you gain a new perspective. A good general rule is to try to switch instructors every ten lessons or so.

TIPPING

Many people are not sure if it is customary to tip for a lesson, but they want to do the proper thing. In general, tipping is not expected but is certainly appreciated. Our personal feeling is you should tip for any good lesson, and not tip for a disappointing lesson.

- **How good was the lesson?** If the lesson built your confidence and skills and the instructor was enjoyable and patient, give a tip.

- **How much did you pay for the lesson (group or private)?** Often, people tip for the more expensive private lessons and not for group lessons. Instructors generally make less teaching group lessons. For us, the rule is that if you got the quality of a private in a group lesson, tip as if you had taken a private.

- **Are you going to work with this person in the future?** If someone is good enough to request for a second lesson, a tip is in order. The instructor will know that you appreciated the style and pace of the lesson so you get the same experience the next time.

- **How much do you want to spend?** If a big tip isn't in your budget, be sure to express your sincere thanks. If the lesson was exceptional, write a letter of appreciation to the ski school. Twenty percent of the lesson cost is common if you were pleased. Tip more if you want to.

When Jeff was learning how to race, he would tip any coach who gave him exceptional information. (He was too poor to tip for average information.) The result was that his better coaches knew he respected their knowledge and would often go to extremes to help him ski better. His learning curve was much quicker than the competition's.

Ask Anna

Q: WHEN do I actually hand over the money? Is it important to be discreet?

A: The usual time to tip an instructor, assuming you've decided to do so, is at the end of the lesson as the instructor is wrapping things up and saying goodbye. Tipping is acceptable, and therefore it isn't necessary to be discreet. If it makes you feel more comfortable, however, it's fine.

Keep in mind that there are other ways to tip an instructor than just handing over money. Money is always appreciated, but if you have really enjoyed the company of the instructor, inviting him or her to lunch or dinner may serve to prolong the learning experience and may be truly appreciated by the instructor. I have also had clients give me gifts, such as chocolates from the local mountain shop, that I found very flattering. It is always good to know that a client valued my help enough to take time to do something special to say thank you.

chapter 7

Getting the Right Ski Tune

"What we're trying to do... is be as fine-tuned and honed-in on the small things as we can possibly be."
- Reggie Sanders, St. Louis Cardinals Left Fielder

Some skiers think that tuning their skis will make the skis too fast. But good tuning improves your control and grip. It's similar to having good tires on a car—you need them for optimum control. Skiing with a bad tune would be like driving with stripped tires. It's critical that the tune is done properly.

Find the right shop. Get some recommendations from people on the chairlift, or drop by the ski school line-up (usually at the base areas around 10:00 a.m.) and see where they like to go. If you aren't at a ski area and want to find a shop, look for what ski clubs recommend on their websites.

To get the best service, you need to know what information to give the techs.

- **Correct angles** – Ski edges are no longer set at a simple 90-degree angle; they use slight *bevels*. Ask the shop to set a two-degree side bevel and a half-degree base bevel. If they will not do these bevels (sometimes their machines cannot be adjusted easily), some variation is all right; side bevel can be one to three degrees, while base can be between zero and one degree.

- **Does the shop use a *stone grinder*** – Most shops use stone grinders, which are the best way to flatten and finish a ski. If the shop does not have a stone grinder, go elsewhere.

When a ski is properly tuned, it should be easy to ski and have good grip. If the skis grip the snow but are unpredictable, the skis are probably too flat. Go back to the shop and tell them the skis are "catchy" and ask them to increase the base bevel slightly.

If the skis will not grab, the base edges are too beveled and need to be flattened. Tell the tech to stone grind the base and reduce the base bevel. Keep in mind that loose ski boots can make the skis feel like they are lacking grip, too.

Some people only tune their skis when they hit a rock and damage the edge or when they put a major gouge in the base of the ski. This will leave you with skis that are generally out of tune and will ski badly and require major work. Shop techs dread working on poorly maintained skis.

Tune your skis somewhere between every five and ten days of skiing, depending on how many rocks you tend to hit.

Tipping for a ski tune is not generally expected, but is appreciated and remembered. Five dollars is generally a good amount if the work was good.

Ski Like A Diva

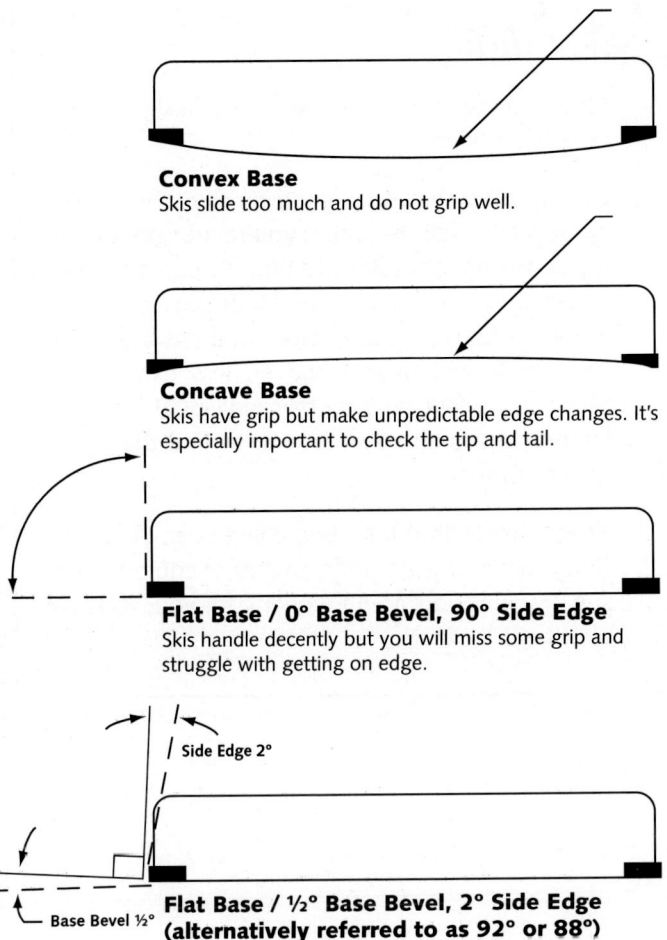

Convex Base
Skis slide too much and do not grip well.

Concave Base
Skis have grip but make unpredictable edge changes. It's especially important to check the tip and tail.

Flat Base / 0° Base Bevel, 90° Side Edge
Skis handle decently but you will miss some grip and struggle with getting on edge.

Side Edge 2°

Base Bevel ½°

Flat Base / ½° Base Bevel, 2° Side Edge (alternatively referred to as 92° or 88°)
This is the ideal setup for most skiers. The skis will be easy to turn and have the best possible grip.

If you're having problems with grip and control after your tune, it's very possible that it's not you — you need a better tune.

Ski Like A Diva

Ask Anna

Q: Are there shops that cater specifically to inexperienced skiers?

A: Any shop that does good quality work will be appropriate. Tell them that you're a beginner, and a good shop will take the time to explain things in detail to you. Avoid shops that process a huge number of skis on a daily basis, as these shops may have high employee turnover, less experienced tuners, and less time to pay individual attention to their customers. Ask around to find the higher quality shops.

Keep in mind that for a beginning skier, your boot fit is more important than any other equipment issue. If your boots aren't working for you, your skis won't work either.

chapter 8

Ski Technique Basics
Simple ways to improve control

"New needs need new techniques."

—Jackson Pollock, Artist and Pioneer of Abstract Expressionism

"The more technique you have, the less you have to worry about it."

—Pablo Picasso, Painter, Sculptor and Cofounder of Cubism

There are some key skills all skiers should know. Practice these with an instructor or on your own to experience significant gains in both control and comfort.

1. Relaxed Stance

Having the right stance is a basic skill that helps you improve your control. When you have the right stance, you are centered side-to-side and front-to-back.

- Your legs should be somewhat flexed at the ankles and knees.

- Your hands should be in front of you.

Find your stance by preparing to jump vertically, either with or without boots. Get yourself ready to jump in the air and then stop and look at your position. In most situations, this will be nearly identical to how you want to stand on the ski slopes.

Good fore/aft stance

Ski Like A Diva

Bad fore/aft stance—too far back

Bad fore/aft stance—too far forward

Ski Like A Diva

If your boots don't allow you to find and use a good stance, see a good boot tech.

2. Breathing

There is an effective and ski-changing skill you can adopt that will dramatically improve your technique. It is also the simplest skill to master, and you already do it every day – breathing.

When you're tense you tend to hold your breath, whether you're skiing or in a traffic jam. The good news is that you can learn the breathing skill in one run and use it for the rest of your life with clear results.

At the start of every turn, *take in a deep breath of air*. As you inhale, stand up and steer into the new turn.

Your breath is connected to how relaxed you are. When you're tense, you take shallow breaths or stop breathing altogether, and your skiing gets worse. By forcing yourself to use a good, steady rhythm for breathing, much of your body's tension will simply disappear.

Note – With skiers at the beginner level, focusing on the inhalation is usually best. If you're still feeling tense, you can add the exhalation, which happens as you finish the turn.

3. Look Where You Want To Go

Your skis want to go where your eyes are looking, just like a bicycle does. Many beginners develop the habit of looking down at their skis instead. Not only is this a safety issue, but it compromises your balance and direction. In order to know where your body is in space, your proprioceptors need visual cues like the horizon. If you look ahead of you, in the direction of your next turn, you'll have better balance and your turns will be easier to accomplish. You'll also be able to plan

Standing tall

ahead for avoiding obstacles and other skiers, and choosing the best terrain.

4. Stand Taller to Start the Turn

You're not alone if you *feel panic before you start a turn.* This is especially common on steep slopes.

There is a straightforward fix. Before you begin each turn, especially on steep slopes, stand up a little taller. Just extend both legs a bit, and then make your turn.

Standing up taller forces you to commit to moving off the old edges and onto the new edges. Another way to think about it: each set of edges can only turn one way (left edges turn left, right edges turn right). The only way to turn in a new direction is to move onto the new edges.

Be smooth with your standing motion, as rushing it will compromise your control.

Breathing and standing taller work very well together to start each turn.

5. Slow Down By Making Round Turns

For many skiers, the feeling of skis picking up speed puts them in a panic. This is understandable, as too much speed can be dangerous to both your body and your confidence. Avoid this by practicing turning across and up the hill, so that your turns are round and gravity helps you slow down at the end of each turn.

Start by slowing yourself more than you need. Use a slope that you find moderately steep, preferably one that is groomed and fairly wide. Point your skis down the hill, then across, and then continue the turn until you're pointing back up the hill and your skis have come to a complete stop. As you get more comfortable, begin linking your turns, so that

Incomplete turn

Ski Like A Diva

Complete turn

you start your next turn a bit *before* you come to a stop. Don't rush your turns; keep them smooth and round.

You might find that if you turn across the hill like this, starting the next turn is more difficult than if you short-change the turn. You already know what to do about it – use your breathing technique! The turn and breath will come together to equal control.

6. Squash the Bug

Sometimes, a little extra edge grip can make all the difference to your level of control. Get a grip by "squashing the bug."

- As you enter a turn, pretend you're stepping on a bug with your outside foot. (If you're turning left, use the right foot.)

- Slowly twist that foot into the snow, so that your knee turns a bit into the turn.

With some practice, you should feel more grip and control.

Note – After you've mastered the squash with the outside foot, you can try to do the squash with both feet. Be sure to squash both feet in the same direction.

Putting it all together

PUTTING IT TOGETHER

Now that you have the five parts of how to gain more control over your skiing, here's how it fits together. As you get more comfortable with each skill, you'll notice that your body will engage whichever is most appropriate at a given time, keeping your brain out of it.

1. Get into a good stance (legs flexed and hands in front of you).

2. Breathe in and stand taller.

3. Start the turn.

4. Slowly squash the bug (for extra grip and control).

5. Exhale as you keep turning across the hill, until you're turning slightly more than you think necessary.

6. Repeat.

Finally, take some lessons. There is no replacement for having a trained eye watch you ski.

Ask Anna

Q: What is the absolute best way to control my speed?

A: Pay attention to the shape of your turns, and how gravity can assist you in slowing down. C-shaped turns will control your speed better than S-shaped turns, and with less effort and more efficiency than Z-shaped turns. A C-shaped turn is one that is round and full, and turns back up the hill at the end of the turn; this is the point where gravity helps you scrub your speed. Once you're comfortable with the speed, then you can point your skis back down the hill to start the next C-shaped turn.

chapter

The Man Section
How to Ski With Your Wife or Girlfriend and Both Love It

"Don't rush me sonny. You rush a miracle man, you get rotten miracles."

– Miracle Max, character from the movie, *The Princess Bride*

In this section, we show spouses, partners and significant others how to be supportive to your skiing needs. (The word is that they need the help!) *We're making the assumption that it is the male of the couple who is the more experienced skier.* Of course this isn't always the case. If you are the half of the couple wanting to get your spouse or partner out there, the same tips apply.

Many of you have seen your share of frustration or had the conversation about choosing a beach rather than a ski vacation. As we know, there is no single answer or technique to magically create happy skiing, but there is hope. A few key strategies can greatly improve everyone's experience.

1. Safe Start

The place to start is with physical safety – without it, no one wants to ski. Help everyone find a comfort level with handling the challenges of the mountain.

- **Start on easier slopes** – Know the terrain of the mountain, and how to avoid terrain that is physically dangerous to either of you.

- **Stick with small challenges** – The quickest way to destroy someone's confidence is to give them more than they can handle. Avoid this by taking your time and by sticking with smaller challenges that have clear results.

- **WHEN IN DOUBT, DON'T** – This one is a biggie. If you are unsure whether your partner can handle a new challenge, don't do it! Either find a way to make the challenge a little smaller, get an instructor, or stay away from that area.

- **Get professional help** – Too often, husbands try to teach their wives how to ski, and the results are generally awful. Both are frustrated and angry, and nobody gets the hoped-for results. Rather than risk the après ski argument, hire a professional instructor.

- **Don't be in a hurry** – Accidents occur when someone is being rushed.

2. Build Confidence

Women are usually better skiers than they think they are. They may not be perfect, which is where the bar is set. Instead of starting with a skill focus, start with building confidence.

- **Cheer every accomplishment** – Don't wait for the back flip to offer some celebratory encouragement. If she skis five bumps and looks good, tell her!

- **Positive feedback** – Negative feedback rarely gets great results. Instead, stay positive. When you both revel in what's working, you both win. Think of yourself as a teammate, not as a competitor.

Ski Like A Diva

- **Don't be in a hurry** – Not only does hurrying cause accidents, it can ruin everyone's mood. The fact is that no one likes following someone who is rushed. If you catch yourself in this mood, just try to calm down a little and move to a slower pace.

- **Admit you're wrong, and back off** – If you push her a little too far, admit it. Figure out how you're going to avoid making that mistake again, and tell her. Remember our motto for safety – *When in doubt, don't!*

3. Pay Attention

- **Don't be in a hurry** – This advice works everywhere! By taking your time, you can focus better on conversations and the time you have together. While this may not give you the maximum number of runs, you'll have more fun as a couple. The result: more skiing in the future.

- **What does *she* want to do?** – If the answer is that she wants to do something other than ski, be flexible. You want her to enjoy the vacation and be willing to do it again someday, don't you?

- **Spend an hour or two apart** – If you ski different terrain or at different speeds, plan to ski apart for a while. By taking a few runs alone, you each can focus on your own goals, even if it means taking a break. Then when you ski together, you'll focus more on each other again.

Conclusion

Our hope is that you will take this information and encouragement and give yourself a gift of fun. Skiing is a serious sport, but you can be gentle on yourself while still taking it seriously.

Give yourself the necessary time to find the right equipment, location, teachers and friends that you may need to make the most of your time on the hill. Be clear on your realistic goals before you head out there.

Though you may still compete with yourself out of habit, let it be light-hearted competition.

Skiing is fun, and you can do it no matter what your level. So strap on the boots, grab your skis (tips forward) and have a great time!

List of Ski Terms

BASE AREA – The bottom part of a ski area, which in modern resorts is often very far away from the parking lots. This area usually features a lot of amenities, such as lockers, cafeterias, ski schools, day care, etc.

BEVEL – The angles that are put into a ski edge, improving the ski's ability to turn or to grip. Most skiers do best with a two-degree side bevel and a half-degree base bevel.

HIGH SPEED LIFT – Sometimes called detachable chairlifts, they run quickly up the mountain (so you get more runs in), but run slower at the staging areas (so it's easier to get on and off the lift). They usually carry four or six passengers.

RADIUS – Related to the hourglass shape of a ski (see shaped skis or sidecut), the radius measures how tight a turn a ski will make. Most readers will want skis featuring a radius between 12 and 15 meters. A smaller number indicates a tighter turn.

SHAPED SKIS – These skis feature an hourglass shape that allows them to ski better and turn easier.

SIDECUT – How much hourglass shape a ski has. Greater sidecuts mean the skis can generally turn more sharply.

WAIST – How wide a ski is in its middle, measured in millimeters. In general, narrow-waisted skis are good for ice, while wider-waisted skis float better in soft snow. Most readers of this book will want skis with waists between 68 and 78 millimeters. (These mid-waist widths are usually the friendliest for all-around use.)